A Thrilling Cookbook for Peanut Butter Lovers

Peanut Butter Recipes for your Incredible Addiction

Table of Contents

Introduction

In my career as a cookbook writer, I have always written Cookbooks either because I feel like someone needs it or because I enjoy that particular ingredient or theme I am writing on.

But for this cookbook, I wrote out of a necessity to help myself, and others eventually.

On a certain afternoon while I was lounging around at home doing nothing, I was actually on vacation in my home (yes, you read right. I vacation in my house. Lol!)

A craving to cook something with peanut butter started and because I was in a hibernation mode, I decided to purchase a cookbook on cooking with peanut butter online.

Guess what? I found just one! It was surprising! And I thought to myself, why would there be just a peanut butter recipe book online?

This prompted me to get off my bed and start working on a peanut butter recipe book.

The result is this recipe book! This recipe book contains amazing and unique peanut butter recipes that you would thank me for!

Flip the page and let's get started with our first recipe ever, my favorite recipe actually - Peanut Butter Toffee Cookies.

You are about to say goodbye to your regular cookies!!!

1. Peanut Butter Banana Bread

Yield: One Loaf

Time: 25 minutes

The list of ingredients:

- 2 eggs
- 2 cups flour
- 2 teaspoons cinnamon
- 4 peeled bananas

- 1 teaspoon baking soda
- 1/4 cup peanut butter
- 1/4 cup sugar
- 1/4 cup butter
- 1/2 cup brown sugar
- 1/2 teaspoon salt

Method:

Step 1

In a mixer with a paddle attachment, cream the butter, peanut butter, sugar, and brown sugar. Scrape down the bowl several times until everything is combined and the mix is fluffy and light

Step 2

Add the eggs to the mixer and scrape down the sides of the bowl to fully incorporated.

Step 3

Add the peeled bananas and mix

Step 4

Add the flour, baking soda, cinnamon and salt and mix until a smooth batter forms

Step 5

Pour the batter into a greased loaf pan and bake at 350 ℉ for 4555 minutes or until the center is firm and springs back to the touch.

Step 6

Allow the bread to cool in the pan for 15 minutes and then flip onto a cooling rack. Wrap and store at the room temperature for up to a week or can be frozen for up to three months.

2. Chocolate Peanut Butter Cupcakes

Yield: 36 cupcakes

Time: 50 minutes

The list of chocolate cupcakes ingredients:

- 1 1/2 teaspoons vanilla
- 1 1/2 cups buttermilk
- 3 1/2 cups sugar
- 3/4 teaspoon baking powder

- 3/4 cup oil
- 1/3 teaspoon salt
- 3 1/2 cups flour
- 3 1/4 cups cocoa powder
- 3 eggs
- 1/2 cup peanut butter
- 1 1/2 cups coffee
- 1 tablespoon baking soda

Method:

Step 1

In a mixer with a whisk attachment, combine all the dry ingredients and mix.

Step 2

In a separate bowl, mix the buttermilk, eggs, vanilla and oil. Slowly add this mixture to the dries, scraping down the bowl as needed.

Step 3

Lastly, add the coffee. The mix will be more liquid than a regular cake batter but that is okay!

Step 4

Using an ice cream scoop or a large spoon, scoop the batter into a lined cupcake pan so that the cupcake liners are halfway full. Bake at 350 °F for 2024 minutes then allow the cupcakes to cool in the pan.

Step 5

Once the cupcakes have cooled, use an apple corer to remove the center of the cupcake by sticking it straight into the center of the cupcakes, pulling out the cake.

Step 6

Fill the center hole of the cupcakes with the peanut butter, you can either use a spoon to put the peanut butter into the hole or a piping bag will also work great and be a little less sticky.

Step 7

Ice the cupcakes with peanut butter buttercream or chocolate peanut butter buttercream for an extra rich cupcake

3. Hot and Tangy Peanut Dip

Yield: About 6 servings

Time: 10 minutes

The list of ingredients:

- 1 clove garlic
- 2 tablespoons soy sauce
- 2 jalapenos, stem and seeds removed
- juice from 1 lime

- 1/2 cup smooth peanut butter
- 4 tablespoons apple cider

Method:

Step 1

Place all of the ingredients in a food processor or blender.

Step 2

Blend until nice and smooth. If the dip is too thick, add a little more apple juice until it is the consistency you would like.

Step 3

Serve immediately or store in an air tight container for up to 2 weeks.

4. Mocha and Peanut Butter Latte

Yield: 1 Latte

Time: 10 minutes

The list of ingredients:

- 2 tablespoons peanut butter
- 1 shot of espresso
- 1 tablespoon cocoa powder
- 1 cup whole milk

Method:

Step 1

In a small saucepan or using a steam wand on an espresso machine, heat the milk to almost boiling.

Step 2

Stir in the cocoa powder and peanut butter until completely combined in the milk.

Step 3

Add the espresso and pour into a mug. Enjoy!

5. Spicy Peanut Sauce

Yield: Sauce for 1 pound of chicken

Time: 5 minutes

The list of ingredients:

- 1 minced clove garlic
- 1 juiced lemon
- 1 teaspoon salt
- 1/2 teaspoon red pepper flakes

- 1/2 teaspoon cumin
- 1/2 cup water
- 1/2 cup smooth peanut butter

Method:

Step 1

In a medium bowl, combine all the ingredients and whisk together until smooth.

Step 2

Use the sauce as a marinade for chicken or save it and slather it on cooked chicken. This sauce also makes a great dip!

6. Peanut Butter Truffles

Yield: About 15 truffles

Time: 15 minutes

The list of ingredients:

- 1/2 teaspoon vanilla
- 2 cups peanut butter, smooth or crunchy will work
- 1/4 teaspoon salt
- 2 mashed bananas

- 1 1/2 tablespoons cocoa powder
- 2 tablespoons ground flaxseeds

Method:

Step 1

In a medium sized bowl, combine the vanilla, peanut butter, bananas, salt and flax seeds and mix together until smooth.

Step 2

Scoop into small balls and roll with your hands to make the balls smooth.

Step 3

Toss the rolled balls in the cocoa powder and coat them completely.

Step 4

Store in an airtight container in the fridge for up to two weeks for a yummy healthy dessert.

7. Plantain Chips with Peanut Butter Dip

Yield: 4 servings

Time: 20 Minutes

The list of ingredients:

- 2 teaspoons salt
- 4 green plantains (not too ripe)
- 1/2 cup peanut butter

- 5 cups oil for frying
- 1 cup plain yogurt

Method:

Step 1

In a large saucepan, heat the oil to 325 ℉

Step 2

Peel and slice the bananas very thin you can even use a peeler to help you get them extra skinny which makes for a crispier chip.

Step 3

Toss the plantain slices into the hot oil and fry for about a minute, only fry as many slices will fit in the oil in a single layer and keep turning them to fry each side.

Step 4

Remove from the oil and onto a paper towel lined dish

Step 5

In a small bowl, thoroughly mix the peanut butter and yogurt together for the dip.

Step 6

Sprinkle with salt while hot and serve immediately with the Nutella dip

8. Peanut Butter Dog Cookies

Yield: 30 dog treats

Time: 30 minutes

The list of ingredients:

- 1 cup peanut butter
- 2 cups flour
- 3/4 cup milk
- 1 teaspoon baking powder

Method:

Step 1

Put peanut butter in a mixer with a paddle attachment and slowly add the milk to combine

Step 2

Add the baking powder and flour to the peanut butter mix and mix until the dough just comes together

Step 3

Roll dough on floured surface to 1/8" thick

Step 4

Cut into desired shape (ask your dog what he likes best!)

Step 5

Bake in a 325 °F oven for 15 minutes and allow to cool before serving them to your pet!

9. Peanut Butter Cup Cookie Cups

Yield: 36 cookies

Time: 40 minutes

The list of ingredients:

- 1 egg
- 1/2 cup butter
- 3/4 teaspoon baking soda
- 1/2 cup peanut butter

- 3/4 teaspoon salt
- 1 1/4 cup flour
- 36 mini unwrapped peanut butter cups
- 1 cup brown sugar
- 2 teaspoons vanilla extract

Method:

Step 1

In a mixer with a paddle attachment, cream the butter, peanut butter, and brown sugar until fluffy and light.

Step 2

Add the eggs and vanilla and scrape down the sides of the bowl to make sure the butter is fully incorporated.

Step 3

Add the flour, baking soda and salt and mix until the dough comes together.

Step 4

Scoop the dough and roll into 1 1/2 inch balls and place the balls in a miniature muffin pan one cookie dough ball per muffin cup.

Step 5

Press the peanut butter cup into the center of the cookie ball. The cookie dough should come up around the peanut butter cup but be level with the top on the peanut butter cup.

Step 6

Bake in a 350 F oven for about 10 minutes. Allow to cool before removing the cookies from the pan.

10. Peanut Butter and Jelly Oat Bites

Yield: 24 squares

Time: 20 minutes

The list of ingredients:

- 1/2 cup raspberry jam
- 1/4 teaspoon salt
- 1 cup flour
- 1/3 cup brown sugar

- 3/4 cups rolled oats
- 1/2 cup butter (softened)
- 1/2 cup smooth peanut butter
- 1/4 teaspoon baking soda

Method:

Step 1

In a mixer with a paddle attachment, combine the brown sugar and butter and mix until combined, smooth, and fluffy.

Step 2

Add the flour, baking soda, salt and rolled oats to the sugar mix and turn the mixer on low until crumbles start to form. Try not to over mix the dough to prevent it from becoming tough. Turn the mixer off when the crumbles just start to form

Step 3

Preheat the oven to 350 F and grease or line a 9 x 13 pan with parchment

Step 4

Put half of the dough crumbles into the pan and push the dough into the pan using your hands or a small rolling pin.

Step 5

Spread the peanut butter onto the dough in the pan and using a small offset spatula and then spread the jam on top of the peanut butter. Make sure both the peanut butter and the jelly go all the way to the edges of the pan and completely cover the crust.

Step 6

Sprinkle the remaining dough crumbles over the top of the jam, distributing it evenly.

Step 7

Bake the bars in the preheated oven for about 30 minutes or until the crumble begins to turn golden.

Step 8

Allow the bars to cool and then cut into 1 by 1 inch squares.

11. Peanut Butter and Greens Smoothie

Yield: 1 smoothie

Time: 5 minutes

The list of ingredients:

- 1/4 teaspoon ground cinnamon
- 1 1/2 cup baby spinach
- 1 tablespoon cocoa powder

- 1 banana
- 1 cup almond milk
- 3 tablespoons honey
- 2 tablespoons peanut butter

Method:

Step 1

Place all of the ingredients into a blender and puree until smooth.

Step 2

Serve and Drink immediately!

12. Chocolate Peanut Butter Waffles

Yield: 8 servings

Time: 15 minutes

The list of ingredients:

- 1 1/2 cups milk
- 1/2 cup chopped reese's peanut butter cups
- 1/4 cup cocoa powder
- 2 teaspoon vanilla extract

- 1 teaspoons salt
- 1 3/4 cups flour
- 1/4 cup vegetable oil
- 5 tablespoons granulated sugar
- 1/4 cup peanut butter
- 1 tablespoon of baking powder
- 2 eggs, lightly whisked

Method:

Step 1

In a medium sized bowl, whisk together all of dry ingredients (flour, baking powder, sugar, cocoa powder and salt).

Step 2

In a separate small bowl, whisk all of the wet ingredients together (the milk, vegetable oil, eggs, and vanilla).

Step 3

Add about 1/4 of the wet mixture to the peanut butter in a new bowl and whisk until the peanut butter is smooth. Add the remaining wet ingredients to the peanut butter bowl, whisking constantly to ensure the peanut butter if fully combined and doesn't clump.

Step 4

Slowly add wet ingredients to the dries, whisking constantly so that no lumps form. (If you do have any lumps, use a rubber spatula to try to press them against the side of the bowl and break them up.)

Step 5

Heat your waffle maker according to your manufacturer's directions.

Step 6

Cook the batter according to your waffle makers directions every machine is slightly different regarding cooking time! Top with chopped peanut butter cups and serve while hot.

13. Super Fudgey Peanut Butter Brownies

Yield: one 8x8 pan

Time: 10 minutes

The list of ingredients:

- 1 1/4 cup mini semisweet chocolate chips
- 2 tablespoons corn starch
- 2 teaspoons vanilla

- 2 eggs
- 1/2 teaspoon salt
- 6 tablespoons butter
- 1/4 cup peanut butter
- 1/2 cup sugar
- 1 1/2 tablespoons dark cocoa powder

Method:

Step 1

In a small saucepan over low heat, melt the butter.

Step 2

Add the mini chocolate chips to the butter and stir to melt the chips. Whisk in the peanut butter and then remove from the heat.

Step 3

Add the vanilla and eggs to the chocolate to the saucepan and mix thoroughly.

Step 4

Sift cocoa powder and corn starch into the chocolate mix and stir

Step 5

Add the salt to the chocolate as well and mix everything together.

Step 6

Pour the brownies in to a well greased 8x8" square pan and into a 350 °F oven. Bake for 2025 minutes and then remove from oven. Allow the brownies to cool in the pan and then cool completely in the fridge as they will be easier to cut when very cold. Enjoy!

14. Peanut Noodles

Yield: 4 Servings

Time: 10 minutes

The list of ingredients:

- 1/2 cup minced scallions
- 1/2 teaspoon black pepper
- 5 tablespoons smooth peanut butter (not chunky)
- 1/4 teaspoon salt

- 2 tablespoons soy sauce
- one box (10 oz.) spaghetti
- 2 tablespoons rice wine vinegar

Method:

Step 1

Make the pasta according to the directions on the box. When straining the pasta, keep 1/2 cup of the pasta water.

Step 2

In a medium sized bowl, whisk together the pasta water and all the remaining ingredients. Whisk until nice and smooth.

Step 3

Toss the pasta in the peanut sauce and serve while hot!

15. Peanut Butter Milkshake

Yield: 1 milkshake

Time: 5 minutes

The list of ingredients:

- 1/2 cup milk
- 4 tablespoons smooth peanut butter
- 1/4 teaspoon salt
- 2 cups vanilla ice cream

- 2 teaspoons ground flaxseeds
- 1/2 teaspoon vanilla

Method:

Step 1

Scoop all the ingredients into a blender.

Step 2

Blend until smooth and pour into a large cup

Step 3

Enjoy while cold!

16. Peanut Butter Chocolate Chip Biscotti

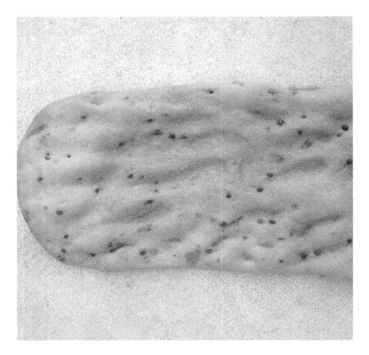

Yield: 24 Biscotti

Total Time: 1 hour 15 minutes

The list of ingredients:

- 1/3 cup butter
- 1/4 cup peanut butter
- 2/3 cup sugar

- 2 eggs
- 1 1/2 teaspoons cinnamon
- 1 teaspoon vanilla extract
- 2 cups flour
- 1/2 teaspoon salt
- 1 teaspoon baking powder
- 1/2 cup chocolate chips

Method:

Step 1

In a mixer with a paddle attachment or a large mixing bowl, mix butter, peanut butter, and sugar until creamy.

Step 2

Mix in the vanilla and eggs and beat until combined.

Step 3

In a separate bowl, combine flour, cinnamon, salt, and baking powder.

Step 4

Stir dry mix into bowl and mix until a dough forms

Step 5

Add the chocolate chips and mix until everything is thoroughly combined try not to over mix!

Step 6

Divide dough into two balls and roll into two logs about 9 inches long by three inches wide. Place the biscotti logs onto a cookie tray with foil. If the dough is tacky, dip your hands in cold water and then shape the dough it's okay if the dough gets a little wet.

Step 7

Put the cookie tray into the oven and bake for about 30 to 40 minutes at 325 °F or until logs are a golden brown around the edges.

Step 8

Remove the biscotti from the oven and let cool for about 10 minutes before cutting the logs into slices about 3/4 of an inch wide. You can choose to cut the logs straight however they are typically cut diagonally.

Step 9

Put the biscotti slices back onto the sheet tray with the cut side facing up. Lower the oven temperature to 250 °F and toast the biscotti for about 8 to 10 minutes. Enjoy!

17. Chocolate Peanut Butter Buttercream

Yield: Frosting for 24 cupcakes or one 6" Cake

Time: 15 minutes

The list of ingredients:

- 4 tablespoons milk
- 1/4 teaspoon salt
- 1/2 cup cream cheese

- 4 cups powdered sugar
- 1 cup peanut butter
- 1/2 cup cocoa powder
- 1 cup butter
- 2 teaspoons vanilla

Method:

Step 1

In a mixer with a paddle attachment, cream the butter, cream cheese and peanut butter together with the sugar until very fluffy and light. Scrape down the sides of the bowl several times to ensure all the ingredients are being mixed

Step 2

Slowly add the milk to the mixer, scraping down the bowl again to prevent clumps.

Step 3

Add the vanilla and salt and cocoa powder and mix until smooth.

Step 4

Use immediately or store at room temperature for 2 days or in the refrigerator for 6 days.

18. Peanut Butter Apple Oatmeal

Yield: 2 servings

Time: 10 minutes

The list of ingredients:

- 1/2 teaspoon vanilla
- 2 cups rolled oats
- 1/2 teaspoon cinnamon
- 1 medium diced apple

- 3 tablespoons honey
- 4 1/2 cups almond milk
- 1 tablespoon ground flaxseeds
- 3 tablespoons peanut butter

Method:

Step 1

In a medium sized pan, bring the almond milk to a boil. Add the oats, diced apple, peanut butter, honey, flaxseeds, cinnamon and vanilla to the pan and lower the heat so the mixture is just simmering.

Step 2

Simmer for 5 minutes, stirring occasionally.

Step 3

Serve while hot!

19. Peanut Butter Banana Cupcakes

Yield: 24 Cupcakes

Time: 40 minutes

The list of banana cake ingredients:

- 1 batch cream cheese frosting (see above)
- 3/4 cups buttermilk
- 2 teaspoons lemon juice
- 1 1/2 teaspoon baking soda

- 2 cups flour
- 1 1/2 cup sugar
- 1/2 teaspoon salt
- 2 teaspoons vanilla
- 1 cup mashed bananas
- 2 eggs
- 1/2 cup softened butter

The list of peanut butter buttercream ingredients:

- 4 cups powdered sugar
- 1/2 cup cream cheese
- 2 teaspoons vanilla
- 1 cup peanut butter
- 1/4 teaspoon salt
- 1 cup butter
- 2 tablespoons milk

Banana cake Method:

Step 1

In a mixer with a paddle attachment, cream the butter and sugar until fluffy and light, scraping down the sides of the bowl as needed to fully mix

Step 2

Slowly add the eggs, scraping down the bowl after each addition.

Step 3

In a separate bowl, mix the flour, baking soda, and salt. Alternated adding the dry ingredients and the buttermilk to the mixer, again scraping down the bowl as needed

Step 4

Add the mashed bananas last and mix until everything is fully combined.

Step 5

Using an ice cream scoop or a large spoon, scoop the batter into a lined cupcake pan so that the cupcake liners are halfway full. Bake at 350 °F for 2024 minutes then allow the cupcakes to cool in the pan.

Buttercream Method:

Step 1

In a mixer with a paddle attachment, cream the butter, cream cheese and peanut butter together with the sugar until very fluffy and light. Scrape down the sides of the bowl several times to ensure all the ingredients are being mixed

Step 2

Slowly add the milk to the mixer, scraping down the bowl again to prevent clumps.

Step 3

Add the vanilla and salt

Step 4

Using a piping bag with a large star tip, pipe the Peanut Butter Buttercream onto the cooled cupcakes. Garnish with a drizzle of chocolate sauce, mini chocolate chips or leave plain and serve immediately or store at room temperature for 2 days or in the refrigerator for 4 days.

20. Chocolate Peanut Butter Bread Pudding

Yield: 16 servings

Time: 30 minutes

The list of ingredients:

- 8 teaspoons vanilla
- 1 cup chocolate chips
- 7 eggs

- 1/2 cup peanut butter
- 1 1/2 cups brown sugar
- 3 cups whole milk
- 9 cups cubed bread
- 1 1/2 cups sugar

Method:

Step 1

In a very large bowl, whisk the sugars and eggs together by hand. Add the peanut butter and whisk to combine

Step 2

Add the milk and vanilla to the bowl and whisk all together.

Step 3

Add the cubed bread and stir together, let the mix sit for at least an hour to allow the bread to soak up the milk mixture.

Step 4

Add the chocolate chips and pour the mixture into a 9x13 pan with 3 inch sides. Bake in a 350 F oven for 4550 minutes or until the bread pudding springs back when you touch the top and is no longer wet.

21. Peanut Butter Snack Mix

Yield: 8 Servings

Time: 20 minutes

The list of ingredients:

- 10 cups rice chex cereal
- 2 teaspoons salt
- 3/4 cup smooth peanut butter
- 1 cup chocolate chips

- 2 cups salted peanuts
- 2 teaspoons vanilla
- 2 cups pretzels
- 2 cups sifted powdered sugar
- 1 1/2 cups mini chocolate chips
- 1 cup peanut butter chips
- 1/2 stick melted butter

Method:

Step 1

In a large bowl, melt the chocolate, peanut butter, and salt together over a double boiler. Whisk together until smooth.

Step 2

Whisk in the melted butter and vanilla once off the heat

Step 3

Place the chex cereal in a very large bowl and pour the melted chocolate mix over the cereal. Mix together well to make sure the cereal is completely coated in the chocolate mix.

Step 4

Let the cereal cool for about 5 minutes and then transfer to a new large bowl.

Step 5

Toss the powdered sugar into the bowl with the chocolate coated cereal and mix together so that the sugar coats the cereal completely.

Step 6

Spread the cereal onto a sheet pan and let cool for about 2 hours before breaking into smaller pieces (the cereal will stick together so you will want to try to break it back into small, bite size sections).

Step 7

Add the pretzels, chocolate chips, peanut butter chips and peanuts to the cereal and mix everything well. Serve and enjoy!

22. Carnival Peanut Butter Bananas

Yield: 4 Servings

Time: 15 minutes

The list of ingredients:

- 1/4 cup mini chocolate chips
- 4 peeled bananas
- 1/4 cup peanut butter
- 1/4 cup mini marshmallows

Method:

Step 1

Lay 4 pieces of aluminum foil that are about double the size of the banana on a clean surface.

Step 2

Slice each banana lengthwise but do not cut all the way though, you want to just split the banana open in order to stuff it. Move each banana to the center of a piece of foil.

Step 3

Stuff each banana with chocolate chips making sure each banana has chocolate chips from top to bottom. Then, do the same with the mini marshmallows so each banana is full.

Step 4

Place the bananas and foil onto a sheet tray and under a 500 ℉ broiler for about 6 minutes or until the marshmallows begin to toast.

Step 5

Remove from the oven and spread with the peanut butter. Serve in the foil while hot!

23. Peanut Butter Stuffed Chocolate Chip Cookies

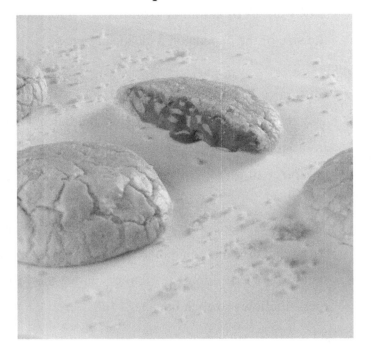

Yield: 36 Cookies

Time: 35 Minutes

The list of ingredients:

- 2 eggs
- 1 1/2 cups peanut butter
- 1 cup butter

- 3 cups chocolate chips
- 1 teaspoon baking soda
- 2 cups brown sugar (packed)
- 3 cups flour
- 1/2 teaspoon salt
- 1 tablespoon vanilla extract

Method:

Step 1

Scoop the peanut butter into 36 small balls and freeze.

Step 2

In a mixer with a paddle attachment, cream the butter and brown sugar until fluffy and light

Step 3

Add the eggs and vanilla slowly, scraping down the bowl to make sure everything is fully combined

Step 4

Add the flour, baking soda and salt and mix until the cookie dough comes together (scrape down the bowl at least once to incorporate all the ingredients)

Step 5

Add the chocolate chips at the end until just combined

Step 6

Scoop half the cookie dough into small balls and put onto a foil lined sheet pan. Press a frozen peanut butter ball into the center of the cookie dough and then top with another scoop of cookie dough to completely cover the peanut butter center.

Step 7

Bake in a 350 F oven for 1516 minutes or until the edges brown and the cookie centers are just set.

24. Peanut Butter Buttercream

Yield: Frosting for 24 cupcakes or one 6" Cake

Time: 15 minutes

The list of ingredients:

- 1 cup peanut butter
- 4 cups powdered sugar
- 1/4 teaspoon salt
- 2 tablespoons milk

- 2 teaspoons vanilla
- 1 cup butter
- 1/2 cup cream cheese

Method:

Step 1

In a mixer with a paddle attachment, cream the butter, cream cheese and peanut butter together with the sugar until very fluffy and light. Scrape down the sides of the bowl several times to ensure all the ingredients are being mixed

Step 2

Slowly add the milk to the mixer, scraping down the bowl again to prevent clumps.

Step 3

Add the vanilla and salt

Step 4

Use immediately or store at room temperature for 2 days or in the refrigerator for 6 days.

25. Peanut Butter Hot Cocoa

Yield: 4 cups or cocoa

Time: 10 minutes

The list of ingredients:

- 1/2 cup peanut butter
- 4 cups of whole milk
- 1/2 cup mini marshmallows
- 4 packets of hot cocoa mix

Method:

Step 1

In a medium sized saucepan, bring the milk to a boil.

Step 2

Add the peanut butter and hot cocoa mix and stir until combined.

Step 3

Pour into 4 mugs and top with marshmallows. Serve immediately while hot!

26. Peanut Butter Cookies

Yield: 24 Cookies

Time: 30 minutes

The list of ingredients:

- 1 teaspoon baking powder
- 1 1/4 cup peanut butter
- 2 eggs
- 1 cup sugar

- 1 cup butter
- 2 1/2 cup flour
- 1/2 teaspoon salt
- 1 cup brown sugar
- 1 teaspoon vanilla

Method:

Step 1

In a mixer with a paddle attachment, cream the butter, peanut butter, sugar and brown sugar until fluffy and light, scraping down the bowl several times

Step 2

Add the eggs and vanilla and scrape the bowl down again, making sure everything is thoroughly mixed.

Step 3

Add all the dry ingredients to the bowl and mix until a dough forms.

Step 4

Scoop cookie dough onto a greased cookie sheet about 2 inches apart and bake in a 350 F oven for 1012 minutes or until the edges start to brown. Cool and Enjoy!

27. Rich Chocolate Peanut Butter Tart

Yield: One 9" Tart

Time: 45 min

The list of chocolate tart shell ingredients:

- 1 teaspoon vanilla
- 1/2 teaspoon salt
- 1 1/2 cup flour

- 3/4 cup softened butter

- 1 egg

- 3 tablespoons cocoa powder

- 1/2 cup powdered sugar

The list of peanut butter ganache ingredients:

- 1/2 cup peanut butter

- 2 1/2 cups heavy cream

- 2 1/2 cups semi-sweet chocolate chips

Chocolate tart shell Method:

Step 1

In a food processor, mix the dry ingredients. Add the butter and pulse until small crumbles form.

Step 2

Add the egg and vanilla to the mixer and keep on until a dough ball forms.

Step 3

Put the dough onto a floured surface and roll until slightly larger than the tart shell. Move dough into the tart shell and press down so that it stays securely in the pan.

Step 4

Prick the dough all over with a fork to prevent it from rising while baking.

Step 5

Bake in a 350 ℉ oven for 20 minutes. Allow to cool

Ganache Method:

Step 1

Put the chocolate chips and peanut butter in a large bowl and set aside

Step 2

In a saucepan, bring the heavy cream to a boil. When the cream begins to boil, immediately remove it from the heat and pour it over the chocolate chips.

Step 3

Whisk the chocolate, peanut butter and heavy cream together until a smooth chocolate forms.

Step 4

Pour the ganache into the cooled tart shell and put the tart into the refrigerator until set. Slice and serve!

28. Peanut Butter Chocolate Chip Cookies

Yield: 24 Cookies

Time: 30 minutes

The list of ingredients:

- 1 cup brown sugar
- 1/2 teaspoon salt
- 1 cup mini chocolate chips

- 1 cup butter
- 1 teaspoon vanilla
- 2 1/2 cup flour
- 1 1/4 cup peanut butter
- 1 teaspoon baking powder
- 1 cup sugar
- 2 eggs

Method:

Step 1

In a mixer with a paddle attachment, cream the butter, peanut butter, sugar, and brown sugar until fluffy and light, scraping down the bowl several times

Step 2

Add the eggs and vanilla and scrape the bowl down again, making sure everything is thoroughly mixed.

Step 3

Add all the dry ingredients to the bowl and mix until a dough forms.

Step 4

Add the mini chocolate chips to the dough and mix until combined

Step 5

Scoop cookie dough onto a greased cookie sheet about 2 inches apart and bake in a 350 °F oven for 1012 minutes or until the edges start to brown. Cool and Enjoy!

29. Peanut Butter Belgian Waffles

Yield: 8 servings

Time: 15 minutes

The list of ingredients:

- 1/4 cup peanut butter
- 1 3/4 cups flour
- 1/4 cup vegetable oil
- 1 teaspoons salt

- 1 teaspoon vanilla extract
- 4 tablespoons granulated sugar
- 2 eggs, lightly whisked
- 1 tablespoon of baking powder
- 1 1/2 cups milk

Method:

Step 1

In a medium sized bowl, whisk together all of dry ingredients (flour, baking powder, sugar and salt).

Step 2

In a separate small bowl, whisk all of the wet ingredients together (the milk, vegetable oil, eggs, and vanilla).

Step 3

Add about 1/4 of the wet mixture to the peanut butter in a new bowl and whisk until the peanut butter is smooth. Add the remaining wet ingredients to the peanut butter bowl, whisking constantly to ensure the peanut butter if fully combined and doesn't clump.

Step 4

Slowly add wet ingredients to the dries, whisking constantly so that no lumps form. (If you do have any lumps, use a rubber spatula to try to press them against the side of the bowl and break them up.)

Step 5

Heat your waffle maker according to your manufacturer's directions.

Step 6

Cook the batter according to your waffle makers directions every machine is slightly different regarding cooking time! Enjoy these waffles while they are still hot alone or paired with your favorite toppings

30. Peanut Butter Toffee Cookies

Yield: 24 Cookies

Time: 30 minutes

The list of ingredients:

- 1 teaspoon baking powder
- 1 cup brown sugar
- 1 teaspoon vanilla
- 1 1/4 cup peanut butter

- 2 eggs
- 1 cup sugar
- 1/2 teaspoon salt
- 1 cup butter
- 2 1/2 cup flour
- 1 cup toffee pieces

Method:

Step 1

In a mixer with a paddle attachment, mix the butter, peanut butter, sugar, and brown sugar until fluffy and light, scraping down the bowl several times

Step 2

Add the eggs and vanilla and scrape the bowl down again, making sure everything is thoroughly mixed.

Step 3

Add all the dry ingredients to the bowl and mix until a dough forms.

Step 4

Add the toffee pieces to the dough and mix until combined

Step 5

Scoop cookie dough onto a greased cookie sheet about 2 inches apart and bake in a 350 °F oven for

1012 minutes or until the edges start to brown. Cool and Enjoy!

31. Peanut Butter Dressing

Yield: Dressing for 23 salads

Time: 5 minutes

The list of ingredients:

- 1 1/2 tablespoon rice wine vinegar
- 1/4 cup smooth peanut butter
- 1/2 teaspoon red pepper flakes
- 1 tablespoon coconut aminos

- 1 tablespoon sesame seeds

Method:

Step 1

Whisk all the ingredients together in a medium sized bowl until smooth.

Step 2

Refrigerate until needed and serve with Asian style salads

32. Milk Chocolate Peanut Butter Swirl Ice Cream

Yield: 8 Servings

Time: 30 minutes

The list of ingredients:

- 4 1/2 cups half and half
- 5 egg yolks
- 1 teaspoon vanilla

- 6 ounces milk chocolate
- 1 cup peanut butter
- 3/4 cup sugar
- 1/4 teaspoon salt

Method:

Step 1

In a mixer with a whisk attachment, whisk the egg yolks and 1/2 cup of the sugar until thick. Turn off the mixer.

Step 2

In a saucepan, combine the salt, remaining sugar and half and half. Cook the milk over medium heat until it begins to boil and turn off the heat immediately. Whisk the milk chocolate into the hot milk until completely melted and combined

Step 3

Turn on the mixer with the egg mix and while the mixer is on, slowly pour the hot milk into the eggs. Add the vanilla extract

Step 4

Once combined, pour the entire mixture back into the saucepan and then cook over the low heat, constantly stirring until the mixture reaches 175 F or becomes thick enough to coat the back of a spoon.

Step 5

Pour the ice cream mix into a cold bowl and refrigerate for at least 5 hours or overnight.

Step 6

Once cool, pour the ice cream mix into an ice cream maker and churn according to the manufacturer's instructions (every machine is different so be sure to read your directions!).

Step 7

Once frozen, place the ice cream into a cold bowl and swirl in the 1 cup of peanut butter quickly so that the ice cream doesn't melt. Place plastic wrap directly on the surface of the ice cream and put it immediately in the freezer. Allow to harden for at least 4 hours and then enjoy!

33. Banana Cake with peanut Butter Chips

Yield: 2 8" Round Cake Pans

Time: 20 minutes

The list of ingredients:

- 1 cup mashed bananas
- 3/4 cups buttermilk
- 1 1/2 teaspoon of baking soda

- 1 1/2 cup sugar
- 2 cups peanut butter chips
- 1/2 cup of softened butter
- 1/2 teaspoon salt
- 2 teaspoons vanilla
- 2 teaspoons lemon juice
- 2 cups flour
- 2 eggs

Method:

Step 1

In a mixer with a paddle attachment, mix to cream the butter and sugar until fluffy and light, scraping down the sides of the bowl as needed to fully mix

Step 2

Slowly add the eggs. Be sure to scrape down the bowl after each addition.

Step 3

In a separate bowl, mix the flour, baking soda, and salt. Alternated adding the buttermilk and the dry ingredients to the mixer, again scraping down the bowl as needed

Step 4

Add the mashed bananas and peanut butter chips and mix until everything is fully combined

Step 5

Pour the batter evenly into two 8 inch cake pans that have been greased and lined with a parchment circle in the bottom. Bake the cakes in a 350 F oven for 4050 minutes until the center of the cakes are firm to the touch.

Step 6

Allow cakes to cool in the pan before flipping them out onto a cooling rack. Ice as desired and enjoy!

Made in the USA
Las Vegas, NV
07 October 2024

96331331R20049